HOW THEY MADE THINGS WORK!

IN THE MIDDLE AGES

Written by Richard Platt • Illustrated by David Lawrence

W

FRANKLIN WATTS

LONDON • SYDNEY

First published in 2009 by Franklin Watts

Franklin Watts
338 Euston Road
London NW1 3BH

Franklin Watts Australia
Level 17/207 Kent Street
Sydney NSW 2000

A CIP catalogue record is available from the British Library.

Dewey number: 609

ISBN 978 0 7496 7480 9

Printed in China

Franklin Watts is a division of Hachette Children's Books,
an Hachette UK company.

www.hachette.co.uk

Editor in chief John C. Miles
Art director Jonathan Hair
Designer Matthew Lilly
Editor Sarah Ridley
Picture research Sarah Smithies/Luped

Picture credits:
akg-images: 19b; Ancient Art & Architecture Collection Ltd: 15, 25b; Andrzej
Tokarski / Fotolia.com: 21bl; Collection of the Earl of Leicester, Holkham
Hall, Norfolk / The Bridgeman Art Library: 27; Dean Conger / Corbis: 23cl;
Franz Pfluegl / Fotolia.com: 21bl; Gavin Hellier: 11; Getty Images: 26;
Hermitage, St. Petersburg, Russia / The Bridgeman Art Library: 13;
Martina Berg / Fotolia.com: 21bl; Mary Evans Picture Library / Grosvenor
Prints: 12; Musee de l'Armee, Paris, France / Lauros / Giraudon / The
Bridgeman Art Library: 18; National Maritime Museum, Greenwich,
London: 17b; National Maritime Museum, Greenwich, London / Landau
Collection: 17t; Richard Platt; 5, 7, 21bl, 25t, 28, 29; The British Library / HIP
/ TopFoto: 24; The Print Collector / HIP /TopFoto:8; Topfoto: 19t, 23cr.

Contents

HOW THEY MADE THINGS WORK IN THE MIDDLE AGES

Visit old European cities and you'll see amazing monuments to long-dead engineers: cathedrals. These huge stone churches were built by hand with the simplest of tools in the Middle Ages – the period from around 500 to 1500 CE. In this thousand years of history, violent wars and deadly disease killed millions. Most people led tiring, hungry, short lives.

Improvements on land and at sea

Technology helped them just a little. Medieval machines like the wheelbarrow and the pole lathe meant one man could do the work of two. New ways to farm gave them fuller stomachs. Windmills made grinding flour easy. Materials such as glass and paper lightened the gloom of the past.

New inventions changed travel, too. With better rudders and sails, mariners could go to sea on days when tides and weather used to keep them in port. New instruments helped them steer clear of the rocks.

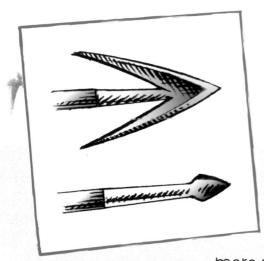

Warfare and religion

However, not all medieval inventions brought benefits. Some made warfare more deadly. When hotter furnaces boosted steel-making, armour got cheaper. This delighted knights. They were not so pleased when new longbows hurled clouds of armour-piercing arrows at them. Even in castles they were not safe. The trebuchet (giant catapult) could pound walls until they collapsed. For the poor of the Middle Ages, the last defence against war, disease and hunger was their Christian faith. And a medieval cathedral was a solid, stone sign of God's power. Cleverly engineered, cathedrals were giant advertisements for medieval religion – and for medieval technology. They still are today.

CATHEDRALS

My steeple is taller than your steeple!

Soaring spires of stone tower over medieval towns. To the people that lived in their shadow, churches and cathedrals were like prayers: the higher they were, the more they praised God. The masons who built these fantastic stone creations were brilliant engineers, coaxing rock into ever-higher and more unlikely shapes, using simple hand tools.

Dark, heavy roofs

Masons covered earlier buildings with vaults: curving roofs shaped like barrels. These heavy stone roofs pressed strongly outwards. The walls that held them up had to be very thick or they would be forced outwards. Windows were tiny to avoid weakening the walls. This made the spaces inside dark and gloomy, and limited how big they could be.

A Romanesque barrel-vaulted roof, used in churches and cathedrals before the 12th century.

Turn the light on, Father!

Where barrel vaults crossed, each had to be equal in size, or the structure could be dangerously weak.

Light and height

Around 1150 masons began replacing vaults with stone ribs that joined at a point. The ribs held up the roof, and thinner stone went in between them. These lighter roofs meant the walls could be thinner and windows bigger. Unlike half-circular vaults, pointed arches could be built wide and still stay up. To build cathedrals even higher masons supported the upper walls with slender bridges, called flying buttresses.

Pointed arches with ribs to support the stone were stronger, and those crossing could be different sizes.

Flying buttress

Can't you make it any higher?

Buttresses (heavy, narrow columns) squeezed the walls in. Flying buttresses supported very high arches.

Beauvais cathedral masons were too ambitious: though they built the highest roof anywhere, some of the slender columns collapsed. The cathedral was never finished.

POLE LATHE

In a forest glade, a whippy sapling springs up and down. A leather rope tied to its end spins a rounded log in a whirring blur. Pressing his sharp chisel against it, a woodturner carves an elegant chair leg in seconds. This pole lathe was a magnificently simple medieval invention. It remained in use almost unchanged for more than six centuries.

How many hands do you need?

Not enough hands!

Turning is a great way of shaping stuff, because it always comes out in perfect neat circles. The trouble is, you need three hands. One hand turns the work. Another holds a chisel (cutting knife) and a third guides it. So medieval craftsmen had to either guide the chisel with a foot, or pay a helper.

Woodchip workshop

Pole lathes produced so many shavings that woodturners made their forest workshops from them. Heaped up in enormous piles, the shavings formed thickly-insulated walls that kept the worker warm even on cold wintry days.

In this picture a metalworker turns a great wheel to spin the lathe another is using. A pole lathe required just one worker instead of two, allowing twice as much work to be achieved.

Wooden springs and treadles

Medieval craftsmen had begun to use springy saplings to turn lathes before 1250. The rope at the thin end wrapped around the wood being shaped, and was tied to a treadle below. Pressing the treadle pulled down on the sapling and spun the work on the lathe. Releasing it spun it back the other way. With one foot doing the spinning, the woodturner had both hands free.

Lively legs

Working at a pole lathe, an experienced wood-turner or "bodger" could spin out a chair leg in just four or five minutes.

I'm speeding through my work.

Metal was costly in the Middle Ages, but almost every part of the pole lathe could be made of cheaper materials — wood, rope or leather.

WINDMILL

Giants began appearing on English hill-tops at the end of the 12th century, whirling their arms endlessly. These monsters were mills, and they used the power of the wind to grind grain into flour. Farmers loved them, because windmills allowed them to stop using the water mills owned by their rich and powerful landlords.

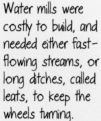

Where there's wind there's a way!

Water mills were costly to build, and needed either fast-flowing streams, or long ditches, called leats, to keep the wheels turning.

If you want to use the mill it'll cost you an extra bag of grain EACH!

That's not fair.

I've got an idea!

Hard labour

Milling grain was hard work. To produce enough flour to feed a family of five, one person had to work full-time at a hand mill. There was an alternative. Most villages had a water mill. It was owned or rented out by the baron who controlled the village and its people. A water mill did the work of 50 hand mills, but using it was costly: the baron's miller kept a sack of flour for each 16 he ground.

Old is new again

Today wind turbines harvest the breeze once more – often on the same windy spots where windmills once stood.

Revolutionary miller

A nameless English inventor found a way to use wind power just before 1200. The wind blew round canvas "sails" stretched over lattice arms. These turned a tree-trunk axle to which they were fixed. The axle turned gears, and the gears turned grind-stones.

Barons owned every riverside spot suitable for a water mill, but mill-wrights could build windmills on any hill-top. This took away power, and money, from barons. It also helped weaken their grip on their subjects – poor peasants who lived virtually as slaves.

Mills stood on posts, and millers turned them to face into the wind.

Dutch windmills

In the Netherlands – and elsewhere – from the 15th century, windmills also operated pumps rather than turning stone grinding wheels. The pumps removed water from swamps and sea marshes, turning mud into rich farmland.

Windmills like this one helped drain a quarter of the land in the Netherlands that was once swamp, marshland or sea.

WHEELBARROW

Why two wheels? One will do!

Sometimes the most clever machines now seem so ordinary and familiar that we can't imagine what an amazing difference their invention made. In 13th-century Europe, for example, wheels were in common use, but only in pairs. Then someone had the idea of fitting a single wheel to a hand-barrow (what we'd call a stretcher today). The results were dramatic...

A two-peasant load

Moving stuff was tough for medieval workers. Long distances weren't too bad: you could load things up on a cart or a ship, and an ox or the wind would shift them. But moving things a short way meant lifting and carrying them by hand, in a lot of back-breaking journeys. Then, some time around 1220, a Frenchman fitted a wheel to one end of a hand-barrow.

Pairs of workers loaded up the platform of a hand-barrow, then stood between the handles at each end to lift and carry it.

This is really hard work!

It makes me feel so old!

Helped along by a sail and the wind, a Chinese wheelbarrow became a "sailing carriage".

Sailing carriages

Chinese people were using wheelbarrows 1,000 years before they were common in Europe. Some had big central wheels and could carry huge loads, or even passengers, because the wheel (not the pusher's arms) took all the weight.

Building a cathedral

Many paintings from the 12th century onwards show the wheelbarrow in use on building sites. In this illustration from an illuminated manuscript, a worker moves pieces of stone.

The wheelbarrow made moving blocks such as these much easier.

A sheep's guts

A wheelbarrow's single wheel allowed it to go up a plank or along a narrow path. A 12th-century Chinese writer commented that, "Ways which are as winding as the bowels of a sheep will not defeat it."

A wheely good idea!

With the wheelbarrow the ingenious Frenchman created, one man could do the work of two. The first wheelbarrows were either simple platforms that could be loaded with bricks, or they had a box-like top to enclose loose loads such as soil. Wheelbarrows speeded up work on building sites and farms, and down mines. However, workers were slow to use them – perhaps because they feared wheelbarrows were taking their jobs.

I FEEL YOUNG AGAIN!

Wheelbarrows carried the load just a little way off the ground, so there was less heavy lifting.

SAIL AND RUDDER

The oceans were the super-highways of the medieval world. Sailing ships were the fastest way – sometimes the only way – to carry cargo and passengers over long distances. However, European ship-builders were cautious people. Always wary of the danger of drowning their customers, they relied on safe, traditional designs that they changed very slowly.

It's the sail of the (13th) century!

Wind and tide

Northern European ships had square sails, and were steered by oars hung over their sides. Square sails made good use of the wind, but they only worked when the breeze came from behind. Wind from the sea could trap a square-sailed ship in harbour. Steering oars were easy to build, but slowed the ship, and could not turn it quickly.

What! No rudder?

Medieval ports often made ships' captains remove their steering oars and later, rudders, so that they could not leave without paying their harbour bills.

Left hand down a bit!

She won't turn fast enough!

Stormy winds from the sea could drive square-sailed ships ashore and wreck them.

Steering oar

Triangular sails made ships more nimble, but needed more sailors to work them.

Now we can sail in ANY direction.

Rudder

Building better ships

Since ancient times, ships sailing the Mediterranean Sea had used a triangular "lateen" sail. Northern ships that borrowed this design could sail across the wind, or even against it by "tacking" (sailing a zig-zag route).

The invention of the rudder solved the steering problem. Hanging from the sternpost – the upright timber at the back – a rudder did not slow the ship, and allowed tighter turns.

Chinese junks

Medieval China led the world in ocean transport. There ship-builders used quite different sails, stiffened by thin strips of wood. These gave crews great control, and stopped sails tearing. Chinese ships, called "junks" (right), had other advantages: their hulls were divided into water-tight boxes, so a leak would not sink the ship.

COMPASS AND QUADRANT

North or south?

Sailing straight out to sea, medieval mariners lost sight of land within two hours. They could see land for longer if they climbed to the mast-top, or sailed from a mountainous coast, but after a day's sailing there would never be anything to see but... sea. No wonder long ocean voyages scared them out of their wits!

Follow that star

Until the 14th century, sailors preferred to navigate (find their way) coastwise: they kept in sight of places they recognised on land. If they were forced to cross the oceans out of sight of land, they had to guess their direction as best they could from the sun, stars, the winds and the ocean currents.

Without navigation instruments, there could be lively debates about which direction the helmsman should steer.

Pointing the way

An amazing device reached Europe in the 12th century. From China, mariners learned of a special black stone called a lodestone. If they stroked an iron needle on it, pushed the needle through a straw and floated it on water, the needle always pointed north. The compass they made with this trick allowed them to set their direction when clouds hid the sun and stars.

Science or magic?

The first compasses seemed like magic, so mariners who used them hid them from strangers in case they were accused of being wizards.

By the 14th century no ship would leave port without a compass similar to this one.

sight hole

Staring at stars

Mariners knew that the Pole Star was always directly north. Its height in the sky showed their latitude – how far they had sailed north or south of the equator (the Earth's middle line). In the 13th century they began to measure latitude precisely with a quadrant. This quarter-circle had a pair of sight holes for spying the Pole Star.

The quadrant was based on an ancient device, the kamal, that Arab sailors used to find their position.

sight hole

FURNACE AND ARMOUR

Rusty red, or polished to a silver-blue shine, iron and steel are so common today that we hardly notice them. Yet in the early Middle Ages iron was a precious metal. It was used only where absolutely no other material was strong enough. But from the 12th century a pair of inventions changed all this – and made warfare cheaper and safer!

How do I look in my new suit?

Blooming hearth!

Smelting (extracting iron from the rock containing it) required huge amounts of fuel. The wood needed for a smelting furnace, called a bloomery hearth, weighed 50 times more than the raw, spongey iron it produced. Actually making the iron was hard work: to get the fire hot enough iron-makers had to pump huge bellows for hours on end. But in the 1400s metalworkers began to use new and better methods for making iron.

Suits you, Sir!

As new furnaces and water-powered bellows made iron more common and lowered its price, suits of armour also got cheaper. However, they still cost as much as a new car does today.

Workers at a blast furnace had to feed the fire constantly, to keep it at a hot enough temperature.

Blasted furnace!

German blacksmiths began building bigger, better furnaces at the start of the 15th century. Shaped like tall tubes, they were filled from the top with ore, coal and limestone. To pump air into these "blast furnaces" the blacksmiths linked bellows to water wheels. Fiercely hot, a blast furnace could completely liquefy iron, so that it could be poured into moulds.

The end of forests

To make the charcoal that fuelled their iron furnaces, blacksmiths cut down virtually all of the ancient forests that once covered most of southern England.

Water power rules

Water power speeded up everything in the forge. As well as pumping the bellows, the water wheel turned a round shaft, from which pegs stuck out. As the shaft turned, the peg pushed down then released one end of a hammer. The other, heavier, end fell on an anvil, bashing the red-hot iron and saving the blacksmith's muscles.

Water power operates the hammers in this medieval forge.

HEAVY PLOUGH

Thank God for better ploughs.

Growing food is tough work, and medieval farmers weren't much good at it. To be fair, they started with some disadvantages. Northern European soils are wet, squelchy and hard to plough. The climate is cool and damp. Only after major changes in their methods and machinery did farmers manage to coax better harvests out of their fields.

Aching acres

We still remember ox-ploughs when we measure land. One acre (0.4 hectares) is the area of land a team of oxen can plough in a day.

Farmers carried on ploughing with oxen until about the 12th century, because they cost less to feed than horses.

Long, slow furrow

Oxen (cattle) pulling simple ploughs did a poor job of digging over fields. The beasts worked slowly, and the plough did little more than scratch a groove in the mud. It wasn't designed to turn the soil right over. Horses worked faster, but tied to a plough like oxen, the harness pressed on their necks, choking and slowing them.

The plough's wheels were adjustable, so the ploughman could change the depth of the furrow.

Harrow

I'm not convinced this is any easier!

Mouldboard

Padded horse collar

Faster, Dobbin, faster!

From about the 11th century, better ploughing made crops grow taller. Improved ploughs had metal blades that sliced cleanly through the soil; their mouldboards turned it upside down, burying and killing weeds. Wheels made them easier to pull. The harrow that followed the plough broke up the soil to make a fine seed-bed. And harnessed with padded, comfortable collars, a pair of horses could plough a field more quickly than four oxen.

Three-field rotation

Traditionally, farmers planted fields every other year. Instead they started to rotate (swap) crops in three fields and increased harvests by half, with less ploughing. Planting beans also made the soil richer.

	Field A	Field B	Field C
Last year	Wheat	Beans	Nothing
This year	Nothing	Wheat	Beans
Next year	Beans	Nothing	Wheat

FOREST GLASS

It's clearly better in windows.

In a wall, it lets light in yet keeps rain out; on your nose, it helps you see clearly; in your hand it holds a refreshing drink. Versatile glass is an ancient material, but until the Middle Ages there was never enough of it. Moving glass works to the forests changed this, and led to the brilliant colours of cathedral windows.

Glass would make this place a lot lighter!!

Removable windows

Throughout the Middle Ages and later, window glass was a precious luxury. When England's Duke of Northumberland went on a trip in the 16th century he took the glass out of all his house windows and had it stored safely until he returned.

Instead of glass, people covered windows with paper, fabric, thin animal horn or wooden shutters.

Scarce wonder

Glass was rare until the 10th century. Most of the workshops that made it were on the coast, where they had a ready supply of seaweed or the saltwort weed. Burned to ash, these plants provided the alkali needed to make sand or pebbles melt easily into glass. But making glass needed lots of wood for fuel. So glass was too expensive for all but the very rich to use.

A brilliant idea

In search of fuel, glassmakers moved to the forests. There burning trees made both charcoal for fuel, and ash for alkali. Forest glass was cloudy and marked, but it was cheaper, and adding minerals changed the colour.

Stained (coloured) glass made possible beautiful church window designs.

Glass ban

Tree-felling to fuel medieval glass- and iron-making furnaces threatened supplies of timber for ship-building, so in 1543 King Henry VIII passed laws to preserve the best and tallest oaks.

Forest workshop

A forest glass workshop was a place of hellish heat, smoke and flame. Glassmakers cleared huge numbers of trees to fuel their hungry furnaces. When wood ran out, they moved on. The forest destruction made them unpopular.

Forest glassmakers had to heat their furnaces to 930 °C (1700 °F) to melt the glass for the glassblowers.

Windows for eyes

Where glass had to be perfectly clear, forest glass was useless. So it's no surprise that spectacles were invented in southern Europe, where better coastal glass was available. Ground into lenses, glass first corrected vision in Italy from 1286.

I can see clearly now!

The first specs were called "little discs for the eyes".

TREBUCHET

I hear they have a trebuchet.

In medieval sieges strong, high walls kept out the attackers who encircled towns or castles, aiming to starve their inhabitants into surrender. So defenders lived in constant fear of the trebuchet: a giant wooden catapult that could hurl rocks with ferocious, wall-crushing energy. Warriors had fought with siege engines since ancient times, but the trebuchet's accuracy and power was something new.

Knights attack a castle while defenders rain down rocks and arrows in this manuscript illustration. Before trebuchets were used, besiegers had to get within range of defenders' missiles to do any real damage to thick stone walls.

Wartime stand-off

Sieges were waiting games. They cut off defenders' supplies, but attacking armies faced problems, too. Camped outside the walls, they had to travel farther to find food each day the siege continued. Some sieges went on for years! Missile-firing siege engines didn't have the power to bring down castle walls, and rain weakened their hair or sinew springs.

Dirty tactics

Trebuchets did not just hurl rocks. In the first known example of biological warfare, attackers of Caffa (now in Ukraine) used them in 1347 to hurl corpses over the city walls. Called the Black Death, the disease the corpses carried spread rapidly, killing half Europe's people.

Powerful weapon

Arab engineers probably invented the trebuchet in the 10th century. They based it on the mangonel, which was powered by dozens of soldiers pulling on ropes. Replacing the soldiers with a weight ensured that the trebuchet's pivoting arm always swung with exactly equal power. The destructive potential of the weapon was unleashed when its operators released the ropes holding back the arm. The counterweight dropped, flinging the missile at its target.

In the biggest trebuchets the counterweight was a huge wooden box filed with rocks or earth, as shown here.

Counterweight

Pulley

Missile in rope bag

Soldiers winch back counterweighted arm

See if you can hit me!

A modern reconstruction of a trebuchet.

Don't try this at home

Carved to match in weight and size, rock missiles could pound the same target time after time, breaking down the strongest castle wall. Many modern engineers have built trebuchet reconstructions and have used them to fling objects as diverse as dead pigs, cars and blazing pianos.

LONGBOW

I'm glad I'm a monk!

Imagine arrows falling just like deadly hail. There is no escaping the hissing attack from the sky, and the arrows' steely tips are sharp enough to pierce armour. This was the terrifying reality of a 14th-century battle. Arrows are ancient weapons, but medieval improvements to the bow made them more powerful and lethal than ever before.

Tin-suited warriors

Mounted on horses, and protected by armour, knights were the shock troops of medieval warfare. They launched attacks by charging with lowered lances – then slashed at infantry (foot-soldiers) with long, sharp swords. Though a well-aimed thrust from a pike (long spear) could bring down a knight, his armour and fighting position, high up on a horse, made him a dangerous foe.

Archers attack

Fourteenth-century English archers used a bow that was longer and stronger than ever before. Perhaps more important than the longbow's size was the way archers used it. Through years of practice, they had learned to draw and fire their bows very rapidly. Lined up on the battlefield in huge numbers, their arrows darkened the sky like clouds. The archers' power turned back the knights' charges – and changed how wars were won.

No ball games

James II of Scotland banned football and golf in 1457 because he believed they distracted men from archery practice. Offenders paid a fine of one sheep.

Medieval knights on horseback used long lances and sharp swords but the archers on the ground could kill them with a single arrow.

English archer

In the hands of an expert, a longbow could hurl an arrow 370 m (400 yd). A careful aim was not always needed: rate of fire was more important in battle.

Length of bow was archer's height

Beeswax coating on string

Leather or horn bracer protects archer's arm from the bow-string

In battle, archers lined up 48 arrows in front of them, and could fire these in four minutes.

Bow drawn to the ear

Bow only strung just before action

The best archers could pull a 90 kg (200 lb) bow

Arrow heads

Tiny bodkin arrows punched through armour. Broad arrows pierced flesh – their shape made them hard to remove.

Broad arrow

Bodkin point

Archers' victory

At the 1346 Battle of Crécy in France, an English army of 15,000 faced three or four times as many French warriors. However, disciplined English archers shot the French knights' horses from under them. On foot, the knights were easily defeated.

Crécy was the first important battle in which archers, shown on the right, helped to defeat armoured knights on horseback.

PAPER

Tearing, soaking, pounding, boiling, sieving, squeezing and drying turned waste rags into something altogether more useful: paper. Sheets of this creamy-white writing material first came from China in the 8th century. When European people learned to make it, paper quickly replaced the thin animal skins they had been using for books and letters.

No more stinky calf skins to treat.

Parchment time!

I can't wait for them to print on paper!

Leather to letter

For medieval calves, letters were dangerous things. It was their hides that provided scribes (professional writers) with something to scribble on. Called parchment, prepared calf skin wasn't cheap: a single beast provided enough for just four or five sheets.

Costly books

Before paper, books were fabulously expensive, partly because of the parchment needed. The 9th-century *Book of Kells*, a hand-written Bible, is made from 340 sheets, using the skin of nearly 100 calves.

Parchment maker

To turn calf skin into a sheet for writing on, a parchment maker first scraped off blood and flesh then soaked the skin in lime for a week to remove hairs. Stretching the skin on a frame flattened it out, and scraping with a curved knife made it an equal thickness all over. Finally it was smoothed by rubbing with a stone (right).

Rags to riches

Europe's paper-makers first started work in Spain in 1150. From the very beginning they used trip hammers powered by water (see page 19) to make their work easier. These pounded soaking rags in great troughs, tearing them into a pulp of tiny fibres. Into this the paper-maker dipped a flat, fine, mesh sieve, turning out the thin soggy sheet onto felt. Pressing a pile of sheets forced out the water. After drying, another press flattened the sheets.

Capturing paper

Only the Chinese knew about the art of paper-making until a battle in 751. Two paper-makers were among Chinese prisoners captured by the victorious Arab army. They were persuaded to set up a paper mill at Samarkand (now in Uzbekistan). Knowledge of paper spread from there to Europe.

On the left a man sieves out paper pulp. Above, the wet sheet of paper is tipped out of the frame. Then it will be pressed, using the machine on the right.

GLOSSARY

alkali A substance that combines with acid to form salt and water.

anvil Massive piece of metal on which BLACKSMITHS hammer out their work.

axle Solid rod that turns, moving power from one part of a machine to another.

baron Wealthy and powerful landowner.

bellows Simple air pump used to make a fire burn hotter.

blacksmith Craft worker who heats and hammers metal to shape it into useful things.

bodkin Sharply-pointed tool used to poke holes in tough materials such as leather.

brass Soft, yellow, easily worked mixture of metals.

cargo Load carried by a vehicle, especially a ship.

cathedral Largest, grandest church in a city.

century A hundred years.

charcoal Black smokeless fuel made by heating wood.

corpse Dead body, usually of a human.

engineers Scientists who use their knowledge to design or build useful things.

fibres Fine plant or animal threads that are twisted together to make wool, string or rope.

forge Workshop of a BLACKSMITH.

furnace Very hot fire used to heat metal, or to extract it from rock.

furrow Groove cut in farmland, often by a plough, for planting crops.

glade Small group of trees.

grain Edible seeds of a grass-like plant.

grind To crush into a powder.

grind-stones Pair of rough round stones, one of which turns, milling anything placed between them.

harness Arrangement of straps that couples a pulling animal to its load.

harvest To collect up fully-grown food plants, or parts of them.

hectare Square of land measuring 10,000 m_2 along each side, or another shape of the same area.

helmsman Sailor who steers a ship.

horn Spike-like growth on an animal's head, or the easily-shaped material from which it is made.

hull The body of a ship or boat that floats in the water.

insulated Protected from heat loss.

iron Silvery metal, prized for its strength and for being hard-wearing, especially useful for making tools and weapons.

lance Long pointed pole used as a weapon in war and jousting.

lens Piece of glass specially curved to bend light, or gather beams of light to a point.

limestone White or pale rock often used as a building material.

magnetic Able to attract IRON or STEEL objects.

magnetise To make something MAGNETIC.

mariner Sailor.

mason Worker who cuts and lays the stones used in buildings.

medieval Of the Middle Ages.

mill-wright Craftsman who made mills.

minerals Useful chemicals, such as oil or gold, dug from the earth in a mine or quarry.

missile Flying weapon used to attack a far-away enemy.

mouldboard Part of a plough that turns over the soil, burying weeds underground.

ocean currents Natural movements of ocean water that flow all the time, or at regular seasons.

ore Rock containing metal.

ox Cow or bull often used to pull a cart or plough.

peasant A poor worker from the countryside who does not own the land he farms.

peg Short rod that sticks out from the surface of a larger object.

pivoting Turning round a fixed point.

Pole Star Bright star around which all other stars in the northern skies seem to turn.

rib Strong, narrow part of an object, building or animal that provides support for other weaker parts.

rudder Flat board at the back of a ship or boat which the HELMSMAN turns to steer it.

sapling Small tree.

scale An object such as a ruler, with marks a fixed distance apart, to make size and distance more obvious.

shaft A turning part of a machine.

shavings Thin waste pieces cut from a larger piece of material such as wood.

siege engine A machine for firing MISSILES at a castle, or for scaling its walls.

spire Tall, pointy roof, especially of churches.

steel Strong metal made mostly of IRON.

steeple Church or CATHEDRAL tower with a tall SPIRE.

structure Strong supporting part of something built or constructed.

treadle Board or bar pushed with the foot to work a machine.

triangular Three-sided.

trough A deep container with high sides.

water mill Mill powered by flowing water.

wind turbine Tower with a rotor at the top, which turns in the breeze to generate electricity.

woodturner A woodworker who uses a spinning lathe to make bowls, chair legs etc.

INDEX